To
Father Ray Brennan
A man of Thought, Faith, Love and Action.

© Patrick McGeown, Pattaya Orphanage, 1993
Photographic Paul Knights, 1993
Inside cover illustration Supot Chawkaew, 1993
Edited by Susan Faircloth
Typesetting layout and design by Patrick McGeown
Also by Patrick McGeown - "No Names Book", 1985.
"The Letters of Edith Clampton", 1996
First printing March 1993
Second printing March 1994
Third printing October 1995
Fourth printing July 2001
ISBN974-89027-7-3

Printed and bound in Bangkok by
The Post Publishing Public Company Limited
Bangkok Post Building, 136 Na Ranong Road, Off Sunthorn
Kosa Road, Klong Toey, Bangkok 10110, Thailand
Tel: +66 (0) 2240 3700

The Pattaya Orphanage
384 Moo 6 Sukhumvit Highway Km.144, Banglamung, Chonburi 20150 Thailand
P.O. Box 300, Pattaya Post Office, Pattaya City, Chonburi 20260 Thailand
Tel: +66-38-423-468, 416-426 Fax: +66-38-416-425, 716-204
Website: www.thepattayaorphanage.org
Email: info@thepattayaorphanage.org

The Pattaya Orphanage

The Pattaya Orphanage is situated in Pattaya, south-east of Bangkok. It all started twenty years ago when a child was given to Father Ray. Today he has over four hundred - orphans, deaf, blind, handicapped, street-kids and stateless old people. They all love Father Ray, a Redemptorist Priest who'll give you the shirt off his back. He's not out to convert the world (in fact most children are Buddhists), he just wants to help people nobody wants. And in a developing country if you're orphaned or disabled your opportunities are practically non-existent.

Today the kids are finding out about self esteem, about love and about being real human beings. And all this is happening in Pattaya, one of the most notorious cities in the world. So next time you're in Thailand come and pay us a visit. When you arrive you'll probably get a big hug from some of the kids and be observed by hundreds of little eyes - don't be frightened, they're as inquisitive as you.

All proceeds from the sale of this book are being used to employ our first full time nurse. For more information on sponsorships, donations and general information please call, write or fax to The Pattaya Orphanage, Thailand.

The secret to reading Thoughts from the Pattaya Orphanage is to sit and ponder the quotations and photographs. Whilst you do this it is suggested you listen to the music you like best in all the world. It is a very personal experience and will leave you thinking about your own life and its direction.

What would you attempt to do if you knew you could not fail?

Dr Robert Schuller.

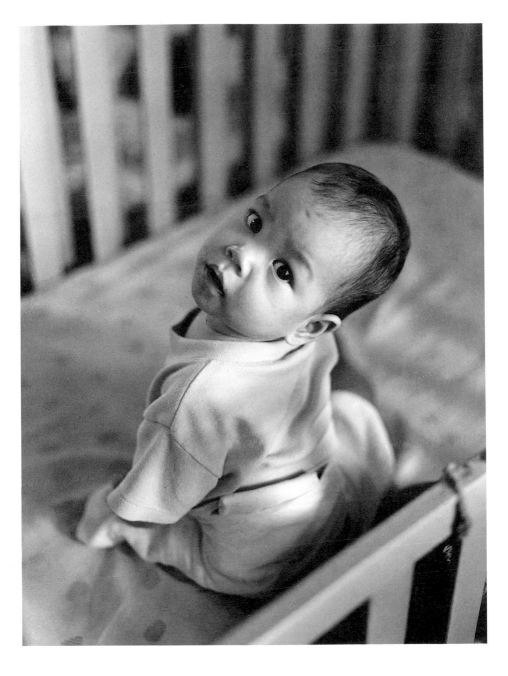

Imagination is more important than knowledge.

Albert Einstein.

If we're very, very careful
nothing very good, or very bad,
will ever happen to us.

Anon.

Life is either a daring adventure
or nothing.

Helen Keller.

Choose a job you love.
And you will never have to work a day in your life.

Confucius.

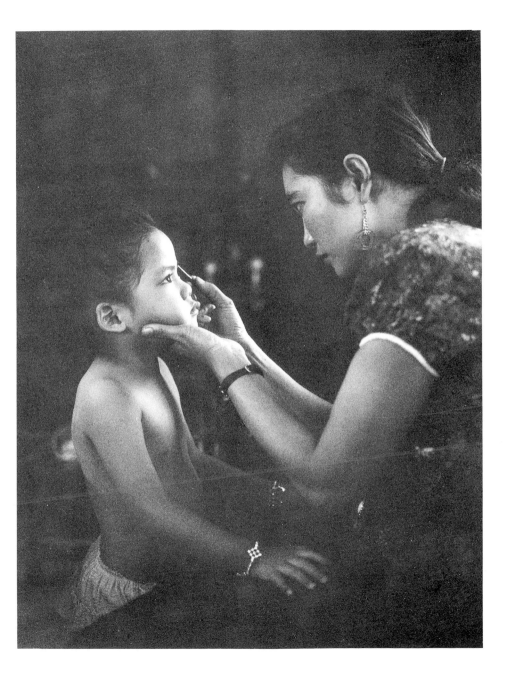

*The shortest way to do many things
is to do one thing at a time.*

Samuel Smiles.

No matter how old you get,
if you can keep the desire to be creative,
you're keeping the man-child alive.

John Cassavetes.

Suffering is a journey
which has an end.

Matthew Fox.

An idea that isn't risky
is hardly worth calling an idea.

Oscar Wilde.

*The secret of success
is making your vocation your vacation.*

Mark Twain.

Never give in.
Never give in.
Never give in.

Sir Winston Churchill.

Opposite - Khun Supot Chawkaew.
His illustration of Thai children,
is proudly presented on the inside covers of this book.

Some men see things and say why?
I dream things and say "Why Not?"

R.F. Kennedy.

He who has begun his task
has half done it.

Horace.

Just because a man lacks the use of his eyes
doesn't mean he lacks vision.

Stevie Wonder.

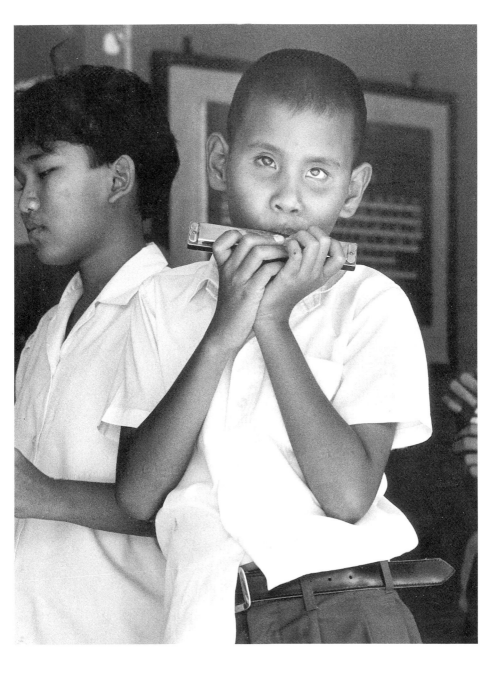

When real silence is dared,
we can come very close to ourselves
and to the deep center of the world.

James Carroll.

*The main thing in life
is not to be afraid of being human.*

Pablo Casals.

Give a little love
and it comes right back.

Anon.

*Every day, in every way,
I am getting better and better.*

Dr. Coue.

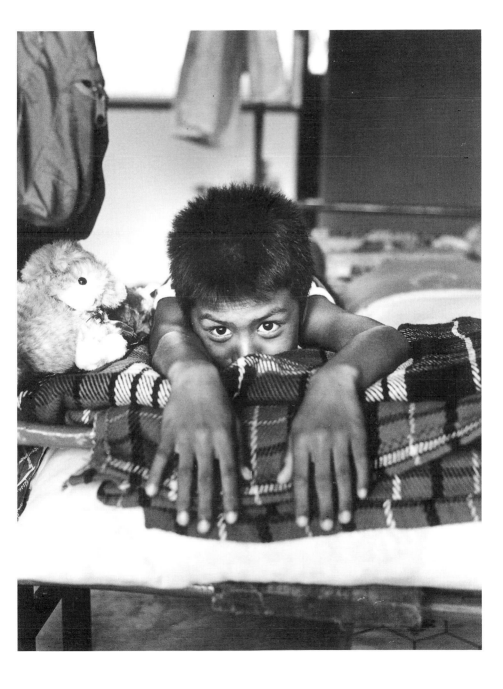

*Everything that is visible
was first an invisible mental picture.*

Catherine Ponder.

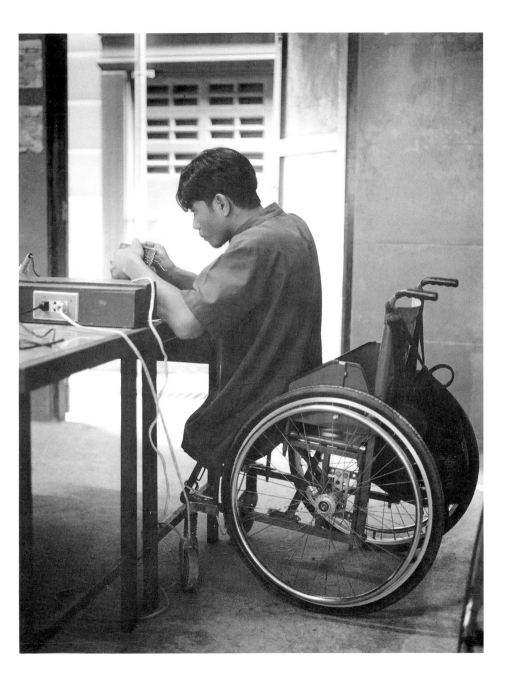

Your body is the temple
of the living God.

1 Corinthians 6:19, 20

Make the other person
feel important.

Dale Carnegie.

Winning starts with beginning.

Robert Schuller.

*Turn inward
for your voyage.*

Angelus Silesius.

If you can't be a highway, just be a trail;
If you can't be the sun, be a star;
For it isn't by size that you win or you fail,
Be the best of whatever you are.

Douglas Mallock.

A peaceful mind generates power.

Norman Vincent Peale.

It is extraordinary
how extraordinary
the ordinary person is.

George F. Will.

*T*he work
will teach you how to do it.

Estonian Proverb.

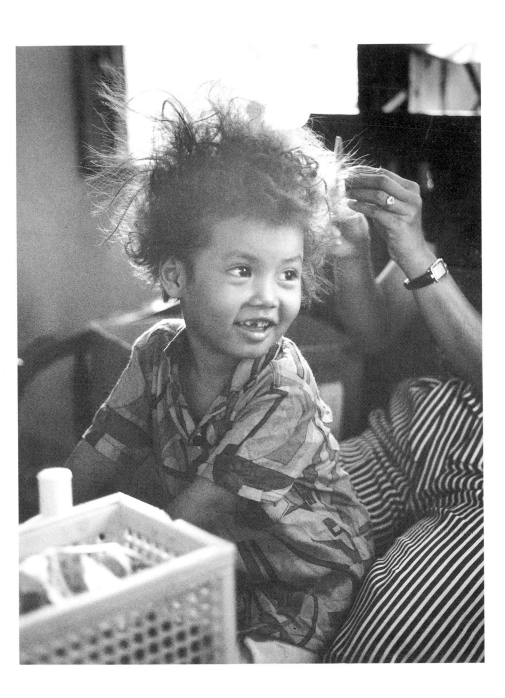

The lowest ebb is the turn of the tide.

Henry Wadsworth Longfellow.

Kindness is a language
which the blind can see
and the deaf can hear.

Anon.

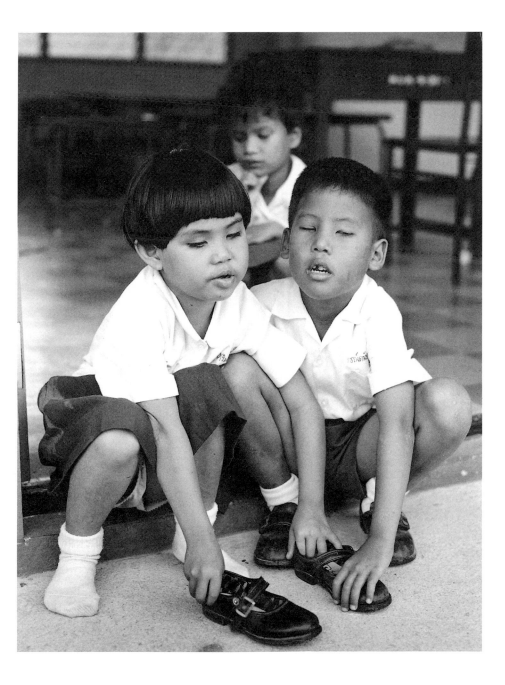

-Just for today -
I will do a good turn and keep it a secret.
If anyone finds out, it won't count.

Anon.

Every man I meet is my superior in some way,
In that, I learn from him.

Ralph Waldo Emerson.

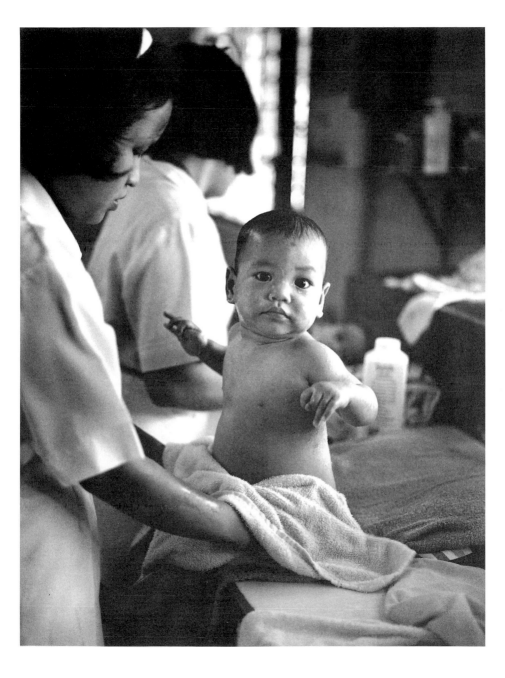

In my friend, I find a second self.

Isabel Norton.

One thorn of experience
is worth a whole wilderness of warning.

Lowell.

A wise man
will make more opportunities than he finds.

Francis Bacon.

Don't let life discourage you.
Everyone who got where he is,
had to begin where he was.

R. L. Evans.

Kindness gives birth to kindness.

Sophocles.

Shared joy is double joy
Shared sorrow is halved sorrow.

Swedish Proverb.

*L*ife is a journey,
Not a destination.

Anon.

Above all,
take it one day at a time.

Bill W.

If anything is sacred,
the human body is sacred.

Walt Whitman.

The very first step towards success
in any occupation
is to become interested in it.

Sir William Osler.

Dreams
are the touchstones of our character.

Henry David Thoreau.

Do all the good you can,
By all the means you can,
In all the places you can,
At all the times you can,
To all the people you can,
As long as ever you can.

John Wesley.

Man is most nearly himself
when he achieves the seriousness of a child at play.

Heraclitus.

Anyone can count the seeds in an apple.
No one can count the apples in a seed.

Anon.

O Lord, thou givest us everything,
at the price of an effort.

Leonardo da Vinci.

Everything in life is a question
of how you look at it in your mind.

Indira Gandhi.

Yesterday's history
Tomorrow's a mystery
Live for today.

Alcoholics Anonymous.

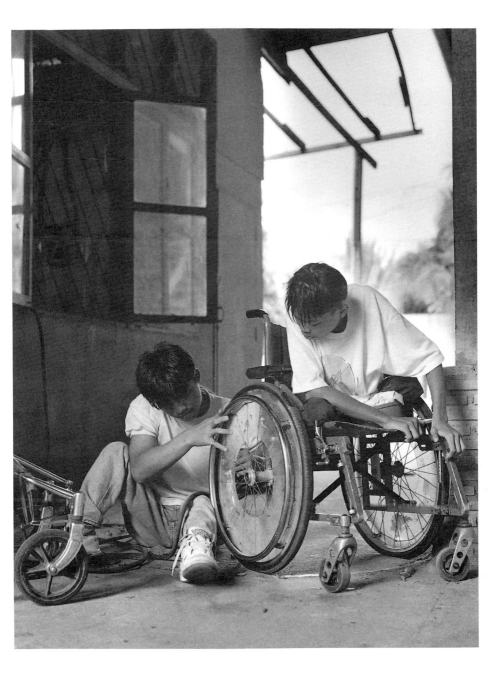

Hatred paralyzes life,
love releases it.

Rev. Martin Luther King. Jr.

The journey of a thousand miles
begins with a simple step.

Lao Tse.

The light is within thee,
let the light shine.

Egyptian Hierophants.

Although the world is full of suffering,
it is also full of the overcoming of it.

Helen Keller.

The greatest help to spiritual life is meditation.

Swami Vivekananda.

Most people are about as happy
as they make up their minds to be.

Abraham Lincoln.

*It's never too late
to have a happy childhood.*

Anon.

*The art of teaching
is the art of assisting discovery.*

Mark Van Doren.

Very little is needed to make a happy life.
It is all within yourself, in your way of thinking.

Marcus Aurelius.

In playing, and perhaps only in playing,
the child or adult is free to be creative.

D. W. Winnicott

God respects me when I work,
but he loves me when I sing.

Rabindranath Tagore.

One cannot always be a hero,
but one can always be a man.

Goethe.

Why not go out on a limb?
That's where the fruit is.

Will Rogers.

Until you try,
you don't know what you can't do.

Henry James.

*L*ive your beliefs
and you can turn the World around.

Henry Thoreau.

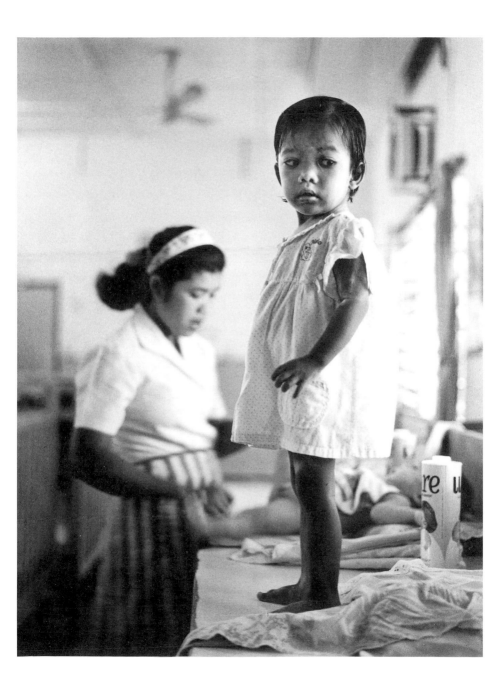

I have learned more from my mistakes than from my successes.

Sir Humphry Davy.

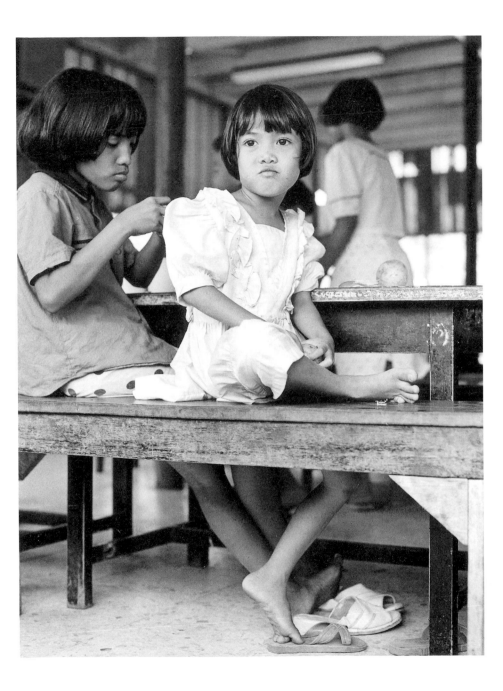

Faith is the bird that sings
when the dawn is still dark.

Rabindranath Tagore.

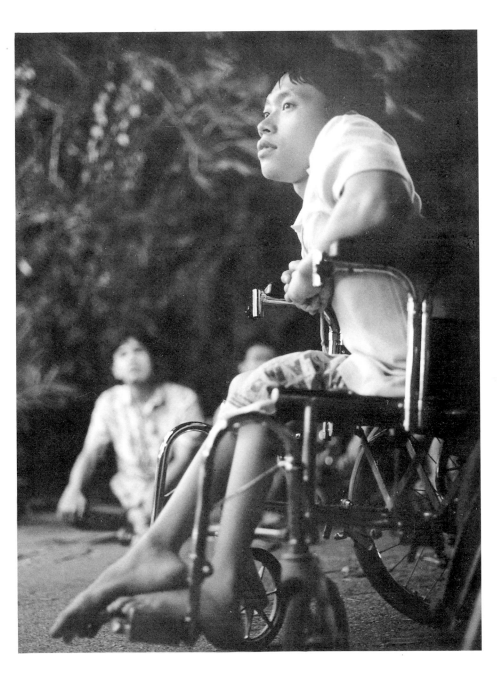

Intelligence is highly awakened by intuition which is the only true guide in life.

Krishnamurti.

If you can hold it in your mind,
you can hold it in your hand.

Carol Marie Guental.

Hatred is never ended by hatred
but by love.

Lord Buddha.

In every real man a child is hidden
that wants to play.

Friedrich Nietzsche.

Just pay close attention
to the small daily happenings,
and gain insight from life.

Book of Zen.

There is nothing stronger in the world than gentleness.

Han Suyin.

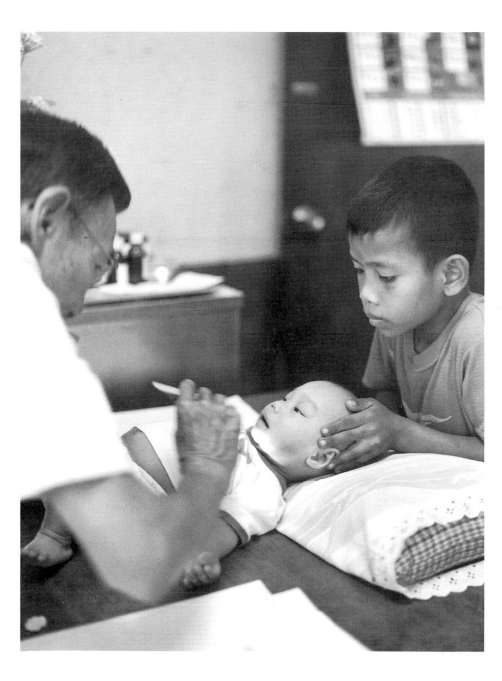

We never know the worth of water
till the well is dry.

Thomas Fuller.

If you do what you've always done,
you'll get what you're always gotten.

Anon.

*B*y yourself
censure yourself.

Thai proverb.

*Vision is the art
of seeing things invisible.*

Jonathan Swift.

*Every new idea is obscure at first.
It is or it wouldn't be new.*

Robert Irwin.

An idea
is the most exciting thing there is.

John Russell.

Children are gifts
if we accept them.

Kathleen Turner Crilly.